T0039885

CALM

Meditations
& Inspirations

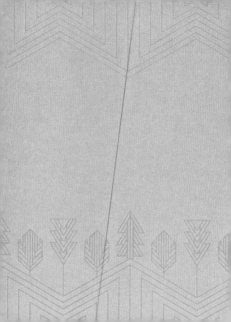

CALM

Meditations
& Inspirations

MANDALA

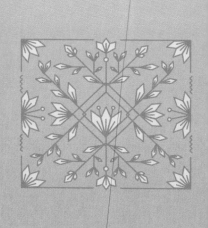

There is
NO JOY
but
CALM.

—Alfred Tennyson

SLOW DOWN.
CALM DOWN.
DON'T
WORRY.
DON'T
HURRY.
TRUST THE
PROCESS.

—Alexandra Stoddard

Patience is the calm acceptance that things can happen in a different order than the one you have in mind.

—David G. Allen

I WILL BE
CALM. I WILL
BE MISTRESS
OF MYSELF.

—Jane Austen

I am a
glutton
for
tranquility.

—Wole Soyinka

Love and
peace of mind
do protect us.
They allow us
to overcome
the problems
that life
hands us.

—Bernie Siegel

NOTHING BUT STILLNESS CAN REMAIN

WHEN HEARTS ARE FULL OF THEIR OWN SWEETNESS, BODIES OF THEIR LOVELINESS.

—William Butler Yeats

You should feel
beautiful
and you
should feel
safe.

What you surround yourself with should bring you peace of **mind** and peace of **spirit**.

—Stacy London

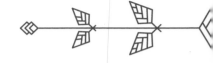

If the mind
is calm, your
spontaneity
and honest
thoughts appear.

—Chade-Meng Tan

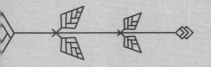

In the midst
of movement
and chaos,
keep stillness
inside of you.

—Deepak Chopra

KNOWING
HOW TO BE
SOLITARY
IS CENTRAL
TO THE ART
OF LOVING.

WHEN WE CAN
BE ALONE,
WE CAN BE
WITH OTHERS
WITHOUT
USING THEM
AS A MEANS
OF ESCAPE.

—bell hooks

Peace brings with it so many positive emotions that it is worth aiming for in all circumstances.

—Estella Eliot

Never think
of pain or danger
or enemies
a moment longer
than is necessary
to fight them.

—Ayn Rand

Never waste
any amount
of time doing
anything
important

when there
is a sunset
outside that
you should be
sitting under!

—C. Joybell C.

Everybody needs beauty as well as bread, places to play in and pray in, where nature may heal and give strength to body and soul.

—John Muir

THAT
PERFECT
TRANQUILITY
OF LIFE,
WHICH IS
NOWHERE
TO BE
FOUND BUT

IN RETREAT,
A FAITHFUL
FRIEND, AND
A GOOD
LIBRARY.

—Aphra Behn

HUMOR
is
emotional chaos
remembered
in
TRANQUILITY.

—James Thurber

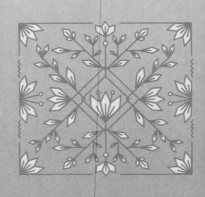

I am sustained
by the
tranquility
of an upright
and loyal
heart.

—Peter Stuyvesant

Even a happy life
cannot be without
a measure of
darkness, and
the word happy
would lose its
meaning if it were
not balanced by
sadness.

It is far better
take things as
they come along
with patience
and equanimity.

—Carl Jung

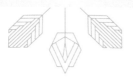

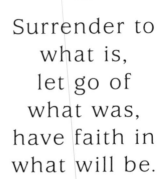

Surrender to
what is,
let go of
what was,
have faith in
what will be.

—Sonia Ricotti

Tranquility is like quicksilver. The harder you grab for it, the less likely you will grasp it.

—Bernard Williams

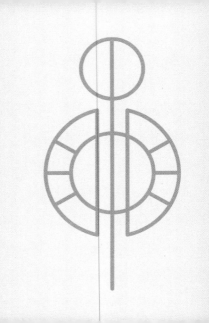

EMPTY YOUR
MIND,
BE FORMLESS,
SHAPELESS,
LIKE
WATER.

—Bruce Lee

Learn to calm
down the winds
of your mind, and
you will enjoy
great inner peace.

—Remez Sasson

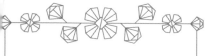

Serenity is
the end—and
serenity is also
the means—by
which you live
effectively.

—Ken Keyes Jr.

SOMETIMES THE MOST PRODUCTIVE THING YOU CAN DO IS RELAX.

—Mark Black

IT'S A NICE FEELING TO **JUST BE.**

—Pema Chödrön

FALL

IN LOVE

WITH YOUR
SOLITUDE

—Rupi Kaur

When we
cannot bear
to be alone,
it means
we do not
properly value

the only
companion
we will have
from birth
to death—
ourselves.

—Eda J. LeShan

FIND PATIENCE IN THE BREATH OF LIFE.

—Ryunosuke Satoro

He knows
peace who
has forgotten
desire.

—The Bhagavad Gita

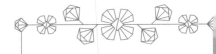

You can
disagree
without
being
disagreeable.

—Ruth Bader Ginsburg

Anything in life that we don't accept will simply make trouble for us until we make peace with it.

—Shakti Gawain

Without
accepting the
fact that
everything
changes,
we cannot
find perfect
composure. But
unfortunately,
although it is

true, it is
difficult for us
to accept it.
Because we
cannot accept
the truth of
transience,
we suffer.

—Shunryu Suzuki

You will
find peace
not by trying
to escape your
problems,
but by
confronting
them
courageously.

You will
find peace
not in denial,
but in
victory.

—J. Donald Walters

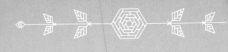

The world's
CONTINUAL
BREATHING
is what we
hear and call
SILENCE.

—Clarice Lispector

EVEN THE
SILENCE

HAS A STORY
TO TELL YOU.

JUST LISTEN.
LISTEN.

—Jacqueline Woodson

I would like to spend the rest of my days in a place so silent— and working at a pace so slow— that I would be able to hear myself living.

—Elizabeth Gilbert

We try to abolish
intervals by our
manic insistence
on keeping
busy, on doing
something.
And as a result,
all we succeed
in doing

is destroying
all hope of
tranquility...
You have to
learn to immerse
yourself in the
silences between.

—Lyall Watson

OUR
PATIENCE
WILL
ACHIEVE
MORE
THAN
OUR
FORCE.

—Edmund Burke

The rigid
and stiff
will be
broken.
The soft
and yielding
will
overcome.

—Laozi

If you are
driven by
fear, anger,
or pride,
nature will
force you to
compete.

If you are
guided by
courage,
awareness,
tranquility,
and peace,
nature will
serve you.

—Amit Ray

THERE IS
NO GOOD
IN ARGUING
WITH THE
INEVITABLE.
THE ONLY
AVAILABLE

ARGUMENT
WITH AN
EAST WIND
IS TO PUT
ON YOUR
OVERCOAT.

—James Russell Lowell

Peace doesn't mean that YOU WILL NOT HAVE PROBLEMS.

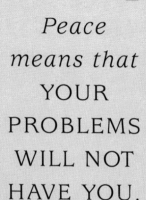

Peace
means that
YOUR
PROBLEMS
WILL NOT
HAVE YOU.

—Tony Evans

CHANGE IS ONE THING. ACCEPTANCE IS ANOTHER.

—Arundhati Roy

NEVER BE AFRAID TO SIT AWHILE AND THINK.

—Lorraine Hansberry

The ideal
of calm
exists in a
sitting cat.

—Jules Renard

Silence is the garden of thought.

—Ali ibn Abi Talib

Close your **eyes.**
Concentrate
on your
breath.
Remember
that you were
not always
earthbound.

—Eden Robinson

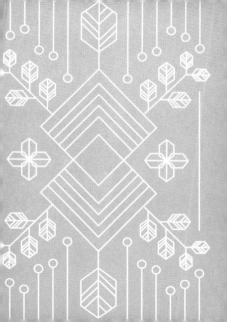

When we are
unable to find
tranquility
within
ourselves,
it is useless
to seek it
elsewhere.

—François de la
Rochefoucauld

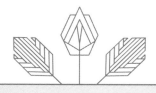

Nothing in life
is to be feared.
It is only to be
understood.

—Marie Curie

The two most
powerful
warriors are
patience
and time.

—Leo Tolstoy

The nearer a
man comes to
a calm mind,
the closer he
is to strength.

—Marcus Aurelius

I HAVE
LEARNED
OVER THE
YEARS THAT
WHEN ONE'S
MIND IS MADE
UP, THIS
DIMINISHES
FEAR;

KNOWING
WHAT MUST
BE DONE
DOES AWAY
WITH FEAR.

—Rosa Parks

Nothing
contributes
so much to
tranquilizing
the mind
as a steady
purpose.

—Mary Shelley

YOU CANNOT FIND PEACE BY AVOIDING LIFE.

—Michael Cunningham

Stay centered
by accepting
whatever you
are doing.

—Zhuangzi

Make things
as simple as
possible, but
no simpler.

—Albert Einstein

Be
still and calm,
don't fear
your past but
use it
for our future!

—Nitesh Nishad

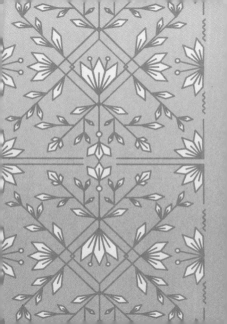

Creative work
needs solitude.
It needs
concentration,
without
interruptions.

It needs the
whole sky to
fly in, and no
eye watching.

—Mary Oliver

Poetry is the spontaneous overflow of powerful feelings:

it takes its
origin from
emotion
recollected
in tranquility.

—William Wordsworth

Not one of us
can rest, be
happy, be at
home, be at
peace with
ourselves, until
we end hatred
and division.

—John Lewis

PEACE IS LIBERTY IN TRANQUILITY.

—Marcus Tullius Cicero

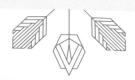

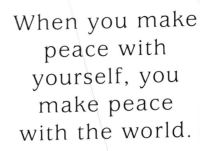

When you make
peace with
yourself, you
make peace
with the world.

—Maha Ghosananda

RESOLUTELY TRAIN YOURSELF TO ATTAIN PEACE.

—The Buddha

Life is to be lived, not controlled; and humanity is won by continuing to play in face of certain defeat.

—Ralph Ellison

Serenity is
not freedom
from the storm,
but peace
amid the storm.

—S. A. Jefferson-Wright

BE
COMFORTED,
dear soul!
There is
ALWAYS LIGHT
behind the
CLOUDS.

—Louisa May Alcott

SIT IN REVERIE AND WATCH THE CHANGING COLOR OF THE WAVES

THAT BREAK
UPON
THE IDLE
SEASHORE
OF THE
MIND.

—Henry Wadsworth
Longfellow

be easy.

take your
time.
you are
coming home.

to yourself.

—Nayyirah Waheed

MAKE
PEACE
WITH
YOUR
BROKEN
PIECES.

—r.h. Sin

Let the mind
calm down
and the heart
start to open.
Then everything
will be very obvious.

—Sri Sri Ravi Shankar

When the mind is calm, how quickly, how smoothly, how beautifully you will perceive everything.

—Paramahansa Yogananda

Everything
passes, nothing
remains.
Understand
this, loosen
your grip, and
find serenity.

—Surya Das

Our anxiety
does not come
from thinking
about the
future, but
from wanting
to control it.

—Khalil Gibran

Peace is not
the absence of
conflict, but
the ability to
cope with it.

—Dorothy Thomas

Expectation is the root of all heartache.

—William Shakespeare

If you want a real experience of serenity, look for the good. Affirm the good. Acknowledge the good.

—Iyanla Vanzant

Patience is not
simply the ability
to wait—it's how
we behave while
we're waiting.

—Joyce Meyer

People
choose to
struggle when
people don't
want to relax.
Sometimes
it is not on
your side.

Relax;
calm down.
No matter
how hard the
waves are, you
will float on
the ocean.

—Kubra Sait

For peace
of mind,
we need
to resign
as general
manager of
the universe.

—Larry Eisenberg

You wouldn't
WORRY
SO MUCH
about
WHAT OTHERS
THINK OF YOU
if you realized
HOW SELDOM
THEY DO.

—Olin Miller

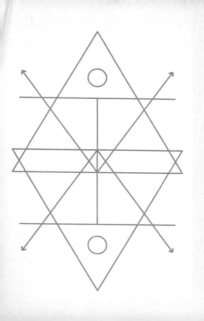

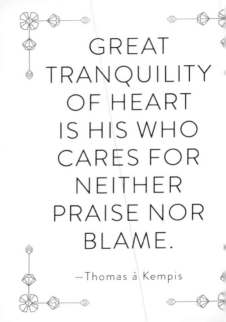

GREAT
TRANQUILITY
OF HEART
IS HIS WHO
CARES FOR
NEITHER
PRAISE NOR
BLAME.

—Thomas à Kempis

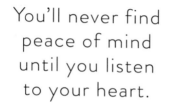

You'll never find
peace of mind
until you listen
to your heart.

—George Michael

If you
cannot find
peace within
yourself,
you will
never find
it anywhere
else.

—Marvin Gaye

Peace is the most covetable possession on the earth. It is the greatest treasure in all the universe.

—Sivananda Saraswati

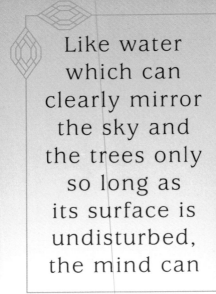

Like water
which can
clearly mirror
the sky and
the trees only
so long as
its surface is
undisturbed,
the mind can

only reflect
the true
image of the
Self when it
is tranquil
and wholly
relaxed.

—Indra Devi

When you
stop thinking
about yourself
all the time, a
certain sense
of repose
overtakes you.

—Leonard Cohen

After a
storm
comes
a calm.

—Matthew Henry

I do not want
the peace
that passeth
understanding.

I want the
understanding
which bringeth
peace.

—Helen Keller

SERENITY IS
KNOWING
THAT YOUR
WORST SHOT
IS STILL
PRETTY
GOOD.

—Johnny Miller

Everything
you do
can be done
better from
a place of
relaxation.

—Stephen C. Paul

DO YOUR
WORK, THEN
STEP BACK.
THE ONLY
PATH TO
SERENITY.

—Laozi

Peace of mind
comes from
not wanting
to change
others.

—Gerald Jampolsky

If there is to
be any peace
it will come
through being,
not having.

—Henry Miller

To learn which
questions are
unanswerable,
and not to
answer them:
this skill is most
needful in
*times of stress
and darkness.*

—Ursula K. Le Guin

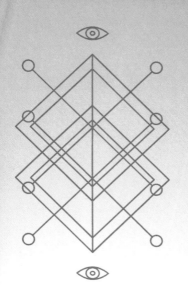

I feel the suffering of millions. And yet, when I look up at the sky, I somehow feel that everything will change for the better,

that this cruelty too shall end, that peace and tranquility will return once more.

—Anne Frank

IT IS THE
STILLNESS
THAT WILL
SAVE AND
TRANSFORM
THE WORLD.

—Eckhart Tolle

There's always going to be bad stuff out there. But here's the amazing thing—light trumps darkness every time. You stick a candle into the dark,

but you can't
stick the dark
into the light.

—Jodi Picoult

Lasting peace
can come
only to
peaceful
people.

—Jawaharlal Nehru

Sometimes when you are in a dark place, you think you have been buried, but actually you have been planted.

—Christine Caine

it's
always
ourselves
we find
in the
sea

—e. e. cummings

My soul
has
grown
deep
like the
rivers.

—Langston Hughes

Like
WATER,
we are
TRUEST
to our
nature in
REPOSE.

—Cyril Connolly

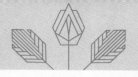

Anybody can pilot a ship when the sea is calm.

—Navjot Singh Sidhu

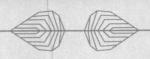

The waters
are in motion,
but the moon
retains its
serenity.

—D. T. Suzuki

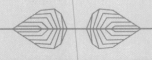

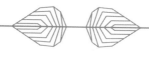

LOVE IS THE PUREST FORM OF A SOUL AT PEACE.

—Matthew Donnelly

There is
a kind of
serenity in
love which
is almost a
paradise.

—Alain Badiou

Know from
the rivers in
clefts and
in crevices:
those in small
channels
flow noisily,
the great
flow silent.

Whatever's not full makes noise. Whatever is full is quiet.

—The Buddha

ADOPT
THE
PACE OF
NATURE:
HER
SECRET IS
PATIENCE.

—Ralph Waldo Emerson

Patience
is the
best remedy
for every
trouble.

—Plautus

Go placidly
amid the noise
and haste, and
remember what
peace there may
be in silence.

—Max Ehrmann

Lighten up
on yourself.
No one is
perfect.
Gently
accept your
humanness.

—Deborah Day

NO NEED TO
HURRY.
NO NEED TO
SPARKLE.
NO NEED TO
BE ANYBODY
BUT
ONESELF.

—Virginia Woolf

HAVE PATIENCE. ALL THINGS ARE DIFFICULT BEFORE THEY BECOME EASY.

—Saadi

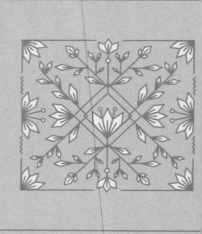

Your mind will answer most questions if you learn to relax and wait for the answer.

—William S. Burroughs

To experience peace does not mean that your life is always blissful.

It means that you are capable of tapping into a blissful state of mind amidst the normal chaos of a hectic life.

—Jill Bolte Taylor

Learn silence.
With the quiet
serenity of a
meditative mind,
listen, absorb,
transcribe,
and transform.

—Pythagoras

SILENCE
IS MORE
MUSICAL
THAN ANY
SONG.

—Christina Rossetti

You can listen to silence and learn from it. It has a quality and a dimension all its own.

—Chaim Potok

I think that the
ideal space must
contain elements
of magic,
serenity, sorcery,
and mystery.

—Luis Barragán

Serenity is not
just an escape,
but a precursor
to acceptance,
courage, wisdom,
and change.

—Bill Crawford

The best
weapons
against the
infamies
of life are
courage,
willfulness,
and patience.

Courage
strengthens,
willfulness
is fun,
and
patience
provides
tranquility.

—Hermann Hesse

From

SERENITY

comes

GENTLENESS,

comes

LASTING

STRENGTH.

—Pam Brown

Most people think
of peace as a
state of Nothing
Bad Happening,
or Nothing Much
Happening.
Yet if peace

is to overtake us
and make us the
gift of serenity
and well-being,
it will have to
be the state of
Something Good
Happening.

—E. B. White

Clouds come floating into my life, no longer to carry rain or usher storm, but to add color to my sunset sky.

—Rabindranath Tagore

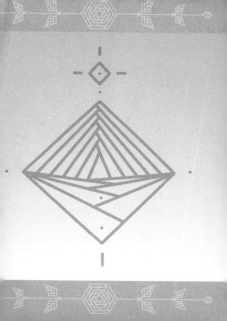

I will fill
myself with
the desert
and the sky.
I will be stone
and stars,
unchanging
and strong
and safe.

The desert is complete; it is spare and alone, but perfect in its solitude. I will be the desert.

—Kiersten White

We live in a complicated, oppressive world with enormous cities and vast populations,

and I try to
contribute by
making it more
light and open
and calm.

—Moshe Safdie

I have learned silence from the talkative, tolerance from the intolerant, and kindness from the unkind.

—Khalil Gibran

IT IS NEVER
TOO LATE
TO BE
WHAT YOU
MIGHT
HAVE BEEN.

—George Eliot

DOUBT
KILLS MORE
DREAMS
THAN
FAILURE
EVER WILL.

—Suzy Kassem

We are
used to
the actions
of human
beings, not
to their
stillness.

—V.S. Pritchett

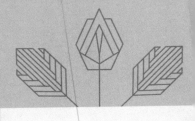

MOTION
IS
TRANQUILITY.

—Stirling Moss

MOVEMENT
IS GOOD
FOR THE
BODY.
STILLNESS
IS GOOD
FOR THE
MIND.

—Sakyong Mipham

Quiet is peace.
Tranquility. Quiet
is turning down
the volume knob
on life. Silence is
pushing the off
button. Shutting
it down. All of it.

—Khaled Hosseini

There are
some things
you learn best
in calm, and
some in storm.

—Willa Cather

What comes,
when it
comes, will
be what it is.

—Alberto Caeiro

There is a majestic grandeur in tranquility.

—Washington Irving

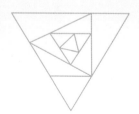

ABSOLUTE
CALM IS NOT
THE LAW
OF OCEAN.
AND IT IS THE
SAME WITH
THE OCEAN
OF LIFE.

—Mahatma Gandhi

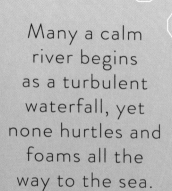

Many a calm river begins as a turbulent waterfall, yet none hurtles and foams all the way to the sea.

—Mikhail Lermontov

if
the ocean
can calm
itself,
so can you.

we
are both
salt water
mixed with
air.

—Nayyirah Waheed

The ideal
of beauty
is
simplicity
and
tranquility.

—Johann Wolfgang
von Goethe

Practice staying calm all the time, beginning with situations that aren't tense.

—Martha Beck

THERE IS
NO WAY
TO PEACE.
PEACE IS
THE WAY.

—A.J. Muste

Peace begins with a smile.

—Mother Teresa

Serenity is contagious. If we smile at someone, he or she will smile back. And a smile costs nothing. We should plague everyone with joy.

—Swami Satchidananda

The mind is
intrinsically
tranquil.
Out of this
tranquility,
anxiety and
confusion
are born.

If one sees
and knows
this confusion,
then the mind
is tranquil
once more.

—Ajahn Chah

I often paint
tranquility.
If you stop
thinking
and rest,
then a little
happiness
comes into
your mind.

At perfect
rest you are
comfortable.

—Agnes Martin

If you can spend
a perfectly
useless afternoon
in a perfectly
useless manner,
you have learned
how to live.

—Lin Yu-Tan

Those who
FALL ILL
of
CALMNESS
do not
know the
STORM.

—Dorothy Parker

Hey you, keep living. It won't always be this overwhelming.

—Jacqueline Whitney

OBSTACLES
ARE A PART
OF THE
JOURNEY.

—Michelle Obama

YOU HAVE TO BE STRONG AND CALM TO OVERCOME DIFFICULT MOMENTS.

—Dani Alves

Fear cannot be banished, but it can be calm and without panic; it can be mitigated by reason and evaluation.

—Vannevar Bush

When everything is calm, start thinking about your problems. When the storm begins, you will not find time.

—Mehmet Murat Ildan

While conscience is our friend, all is at peace; however, once it is offended, farewell to a tranquil mind.

—Mary Wortley Montagu

Being
well-dressed
gives a feeling
of inward
tranquility which
psychoanalysis
is powerless
to bestow.

—Sebastian Horsley

I define joy
as a sustained
sense of
well-being
and internal
peace—a
connection to
what matters.

—Oprah Winfrey

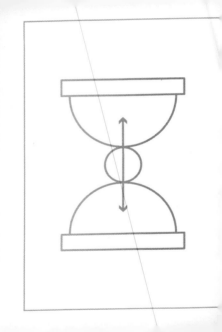

Peace is not the absence of chaos. It is the presence of tranquility and joy in the midst of chaos.

—Debasish Mridha

IN THE MADNESS, YOU HAVE TO FIND CALM.

—Lupita Nyong'o

You find peace
by coming to
terms with
what you
don't know.

—Nassim Nicholas Taleb

The real *spiritual progress* of the aspirant is measured by the extent to which he achieves *inner tranquility.*

—Swami Sivananda

WORRYING DOES NOT TAKE AWAY TOMORROW'S TROUBLES, IT TAKES AWAY TODAY'S PEACE.

—Randy Armstrong

Finish each day
and be
done with it.
You have
done what you
could.

—Ralph Waldo Emerson

Peace is present right here and now, in ourselves and in everything we do and see.

—Thích Nhất Hạnh

Never be
in a hurry;
do everything
quietly and in a
calm spirit.
Do not lose
your inner peace
for anything
whatsoever,

even if your
whole world
seems upset.

—Saint Francis de Sales

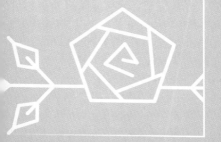

You can't calm
the storm, so
stop trying.
What you can
do is calm
yourself. The
storm will pass.

—Timber Hawkeye

RIVERS KNOW
THIS: THERE
IS NO HURRY.
WE SHALL
GET THERE
SOME DAY.

—A.A. Milne

Everything has
its wonders,
even darkness
and silence,
and I learn,
whatever state
I may be in,
therein to be
content.

—Helen Keller

I don't think many people appreciate silence or realize that it is as close to music as you can get.

—Toni Morrison

YOU'RE NOT
ALONE.
AND YOU'RE
GOING TO
BE OKAY.
BE KIND TO
YOURSELF.

—Andrea Russett

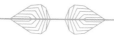

Give your stress wings and let it fly away.

—Terri Guillemets

YOU CAN
FALL,
BUT YOU
CAN
RISE ALSO.

—Angelique Kidjo

The key to **SERENITY** is trusting that the **UNIVERSE** has your back.

—Gabrielle Bernstein

Life appears to
me too short
to be spent in
nursing animosity,
or registering
wrongs. With
this creed,
revenge never
worries my heart,

degradation
never too deeply
disgusts me,
injustice never
crushes me too
low. I live in
calm, looking
to the end.

—Charlotte Brontë

Life should be touched, not strangled. You've got to relax, let it happen at times, and at others move forward with it.

—Ray Bradbury

Learn to be
quiet enough to
hear the sound
of the genuine
within yourself
so that you can
hear it in others.

—Marian Wright Edelman

Life has its
rhythm and
we have ours.

—Victoria Moran

Harvest the
FRUITS
OF YOUR
DAYDREAMS
and rest.

Water and
sunlight to the
BEST IN YOU.

—Lin-Manuel Miranda

MANDALA

Mandala Publishing
P.O. Box 3088
San Rafael, CA 94912
www.mandalaearth.com

CEO: Raoul Goff
PRESIDENT: Kate Jerome
PUBLISHER: Roger Shaw
ASSOCIATE PUBLISHER: Mariah Bear
CREATIVE DIRECTOR: Chrissy Kwasnik
ART DIRECTOR: Allister Fein
DESIGNER: Megan Sinead-Harris
EDITORIAL TEAM: Ian Cannon & Madeleine Calvi
MANAGING EDITOR: Tarji Rodriguez
PRODUCTION MANAGER: Binh Au

978-1-68383-976-7
Printed in China
10 9 8 7 6 5 4 3 2
2021 2022 2023